Front cover photo: Telford Plaza and office buildings, Telford, Shropshire.

Inside front cover photo: Social housing in Skelmersdale, Lancashire.

Contents page photo: The Golden Cross public house and ring road bridge, Redditch.

Rear cover photo: Netteswell Orchard, Harlow, Essex.

Inside rear cover photo: Princess Square interior, Bracknell, Berkshire.

Published wordwide by IngramSpark.

978-1-9164125-0-7 (Paperback)

With thanks to Kenneth Baker

and the Fred Roche Foundation.

© Thomas Walker 2018. All rights reserved. No part of
This book may be reproduced or transmitted in any form
without the written permission of the author.
All photos taken by the author unless otherwise stated.

Contents

Introduction	– Page 4
The Forerunners	– Page 5
The First Generation: 1946-1950	– Page 10
The Second Generation: 1961-1964	– Page 33
The Third Generation: 1967-1970	– Page 44
Outside the Programme	– Page 62
The Next Generation	– Page 70
Index	– Page 75

About the Author

I've been interested in transport since a very early age. At the age of six, whilst looking at a map of Milton Keynes, I started asking myself why certain roads seemed to end in unusual places and projecting how they might continue. So began an interest in urban planning and city design that would shape the decades to come. After spending many years campaigning to get the heritage of "Britain's newest city" recognised, I began to work for local parish councils, putting my enthusiasm for planning to practical use. I also started to turn my attention to other similar towns up and down the country, and in 2009 I set myself the goal of visiting all of Britain's new towns. That's a goal that still isn't quite complete, but this volume is, at least, the first product of that endeavour.

Introduction

The Second World War left Britain with a severe shortage of housing. Many of the country's urban areas had been decimated during the war, and much of the housing that remained was Victorian or older, with little or no heating, no interior toilets and very little space for large families.

A building program was the natural answer. However, rather than build up the centre of large cities with new high-rise development, the decision was taken to build a series of completely new settlements.

The first wave was primarily built around London, outside the new green belt. A later wave followed further north, while a third and final brought into being some of the largest and most successful towns in the country.

Many of these towns share common architectural, urban and cultural characteristics, while some also have unique design styles and eccentricities. But sadly, much of that is now under threat. What's in vogue in the planning and architectural worlds has changed considerably, and the urban form of these towns no longer fits with today's ideology.

Public art in Stevenage new town centre.

This book aims to capture the spirit and character of these often-maligned towns and cities. They are not yet old enough for their distinctive uniqueness to be recognised for what it is. With the exception of Milton Keynes, where civic groups have forced policies through to protect the city's urban form, little is being done to preserve these distinctive places.

The names of a lot of these towns will elicit scornful reactions from many people. Names like Corby, Bracknell, Crawley and Harlow do little to evoke thoughts of beauty and character, and the urban form of the earlier new towns in particular is seen as brutal and unwelcoming by today's standards.

However, the fact remains that these towns were built on a different set of principles to what is popular today. Just as older towns were built for the horse, so these towns were built for the car.

Perhaps that isn't what's needed today, but it is part of the history of these places, and that hasn't tended to be respected in recent years. Hopefully more will now be done to acknowledge and preserve some of that heritage before much more of it is lost forever.

The Forerunners

Planned towns and cities are not a new concept in the UK. Many of Britain's oldest towns and cities were planned and built by the Romans, like St. Albans, known originally as Verulamium. Later, grid layouts were adopted for new settlements in the middle ages and through the renaissance, culminating in the beautifully planned centres of Edinburgh and Glasgow.

The story of 'new towns' as the term is understood today really begins in 1903 with the creation of Letchworth Garden City. This, along with nearby Welwyn, created in 1920, was an expression of the 'garden cities' movement developed towards the end of the 19th century.

This movement, brought about primarily by Ebenezer Howard, sought to create a new kind of community, replacing the dense and busy centres of traditional towns with a blend of city and country, creating urban areas that sit in a framework of greenery.

Letchworth Garden City:

The garden cities would go on to influence town planning in Britain throughout the new towns programme and beyond. Greenery was essential to the identities of these early pioneers, from the leafy suburbs nestled in thick bands of woodland through to the tree-lined boulevards that define their centres. Letchworth did this on a smaller scale than what came later in the movement, as seen here with Broadway, the main spine linking the town's central park with the railway station.

Letchworth Garden City:

The architecture of the garden cities was reserved but beautiful, and a far cry from much of what was to come. A neo-Georgian style is evident in many buildings, shunning the more garish elements of Victorian flamboyance but retaining a sense of beauty alongside more functional form.

Welwyn Garden City:

While Letchworth was the birthplace of the garden cities concept, nearby Welwyn took it to an altogether different level. Here influence was taken from the likes of Washington DC, with wide green Boulevards intersecting at right angles. Parkway, seen here from its northern limit at The Campus looking south, is half a mile in length and 190 feet wide from building line to building line.

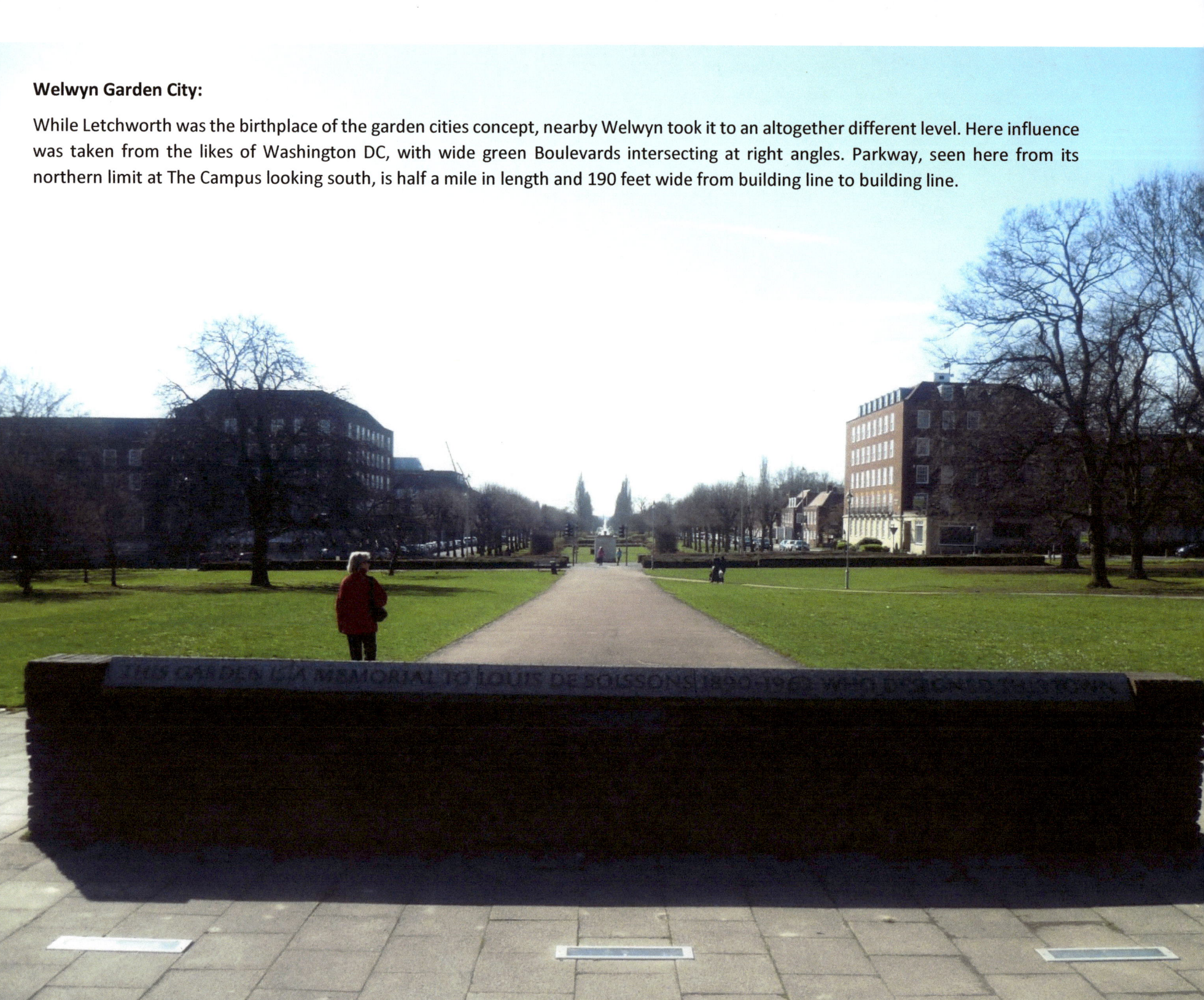

Welwyn Garden City:

The intersection of Parkway with Howardsgate, Welwyn's other central Boulevard, is marked by the Coronation Fountain. The two Boulevards are filled with public seating, monuments and artworks, including a war memorial and a statue of Howard himself.

Between them, Welwyn and Letchworth represent a kind of grandness of vision and scale that would disappear in the next chapter of the new town story, not to reappear until many decades later. The idea of fusing town and country would remain core to future new town design, but these stunning attempts at grandeur would give way to a more pragmatic and functional urban form in the post-war years.

The First Generation: 1946-1950

The late 1940s were a time of dramatic change for Britain. Following the Second World War, a surprise election defeat for Winston Churchill had put Labour's Clement Atlee into power. He would go on to fundamentally restructure the United Kingdom into a country where the government played a far larger role in day-to-day life. Industries were nationalised, public services were created and a large-scale housebuilding programme was launched.

Prior to the war, many towns and cities had expanded dramatically as enterprising developers created 'Metro-land', a network of sprawling leafy suburbs around London and other major cities. With the country now facing a housing crisis, the new government decided to restrict the further growth of major cities and instead focus on a wave of completely new, planned settlements. These would embrace the latest trends in architecture and design, being planned as easy places to live, travel and work. Gone was the traditional high street, replaced with wide pedestrian squares, fast roads and indoor shopping complexes.

Stevenage:

This distinctive clocktower and water feature form the centrepiece of the first new town to be designated. Stevenage was the first of several new towns to appear in Hertfordshire under the New Towns Act 1946, following on from Ebenezer Howard's two earlier Garden Cities in the same county.

Like many first and second generation new towns, Stevenage gained a new town centre in addition to a smaller, pre-existing one. The original high street is now known as 'Stevenage Old Town', while the new town centre has taken its place as the main civic hub. The town's railway station was relocated south to be integrated into the new town centre by way of an elevated walkway, and went on to replace Hitchin as the primary intercity stop between London and Peterborough.

Stevenage:

An early adopter of cycling as a primary mode of transport, Stevenage Development Corporation built an extensive network of dedicated cycle paths across the town. These 'cycleways' are reminiscent of those found in Dutch cities like Eindhoven and Arnhem, but despite the fast, direct routes and wide, open underpasses (contrasting with the narrow and user-unfriendly 'subways' found in some other new towns) cycle usage here is below the national average and this fantastic network gets very little of the traffic it was designed for.

Crawley:

The only new town in the entire programme to be located south of London, Crawley sits in the shadow of Gatwick Airport. This proximity has encouraged a lot of growth in the area, but equally the slightly off-the-grid location of the town centre, located one stop away from the Brighton Main Line on the branch towards Horsham, means a lot of potential custom bypasses the town. Like in Stevenage, concrete is very much the order of the day here, but unlike its immediate predecessor, Crawley did not construct a separate town centre to replace its original one. Instead it grew and adapted what was already there, leading to a more dispersed and traditional-feeling layout.

Crawley:

A lot of new towns have distinctive, unique styles of signage and other street furniture. Crawley is an exemplar in this regard. Each of the estates here is colour-coded, with the name of the estate shown below street names on all signs.

Nowadays, the focus of many local authorities is to reduce the cost of procurement, leading to the bland mediocrity of a few off-the-shelf designs of signage across the country. Custom designs like this are difficult to maintain, and in many of these towns the newer estates lack distinctive and characterful features like this.

Hemel Hempstead:

Another early post-war designation, Hemel Hempstead became a new town in February 1947. Its new town centre featured a wide, straight high street, a park outfitted with some delightful water features and one of Britain's few 'magic roundabouts', with six mini roundabouts arranged in a circle around a central island.

By far the most noticeable feature of Hemel Hempstead, however, was the Kodak Tower. For a long time the town centre was dominated by this industrial concrete behemoth with its accompanying elevated service roads and supporting buildings. In the mid-2000s Kodak vacated the building, and not without controversy it was decided to modernise it into an apartment tower. In the process it gained an extra two floors, and the resulting 19-storey glass tower is now a brightly visible landmark from the Chiltern Hills and surrounding towns.

The new development around the tower contrasts heavily with the older concrete infrastructure around the magic roundabout.

Hemel Hempstead:

Like so many of England's new towns, Hemel Hempstead was an existing small town prior to its designation. The new town centre was built to the south of the old one on an area known as Marlowes. The modern day Marlowes Shopping Centre sits almost directly on top of the original Hemel Hempstead railway station, terminus of the Midland Railway branch from Harpenden. The modern day Hemel Hempstead station was originally called Boxmoor.

Hemel Hempstead:

Gadebridge Park, located a stone's throw from both town centres.

Harlow:

Just across the border from Hertfordshire into Essex, Harlow featured a town centre built on two levels. Starting with Stevenage, this was to become a popular feature of first and second generation new towns, with shops and residences separated on different levels. It was a school of design that continued into the 1970s, perhaps reaching its epitome in the City of London Pedways system and the Barbican Estate. However, problems arose when trying to generate activity on the upper level and encourage business to set up there, especially when the legal status of these spaces was often unclear.

Harlow:

The heart of the new town centre in Harlow is the market square. Obvious attempts have been made to create a dynamic public space here, with a mixture of retail units and residences, space for an open-air market and various public art including the clock motif, to give the square a sense of 'place'. However, as this image, taken at 4pm on a Thursday, shows, the square is quite under-patronised, perhaps not aided by the lack of compelling retail around it. It's not only the upper levels in these town centres that struggle to generate commercial interest. A key part of building a new community is recognising that people will only go where they want to, and businesses will only operate in the way that works for them. Planners in many new towns attempted to design places to shape the way people and businesses would behave, and a successful new town needs to be shaped by the way people and businesses behave to avoid failed spaces like this.

Peterlee:

The two first generation new towns located in County Durham took a somewhat different direction to those in the south. There is much less focus on movement in Peterlee and Newton Aycliffe, with no carefully-planned suburbs or high-quality road infrastructure. Instead both towns are built like large housing developments around a modest town centre. Peterlee does have a few distinctive points to its name though, most notable of which is the Grade II* listed Apollo Pavilion. This bizarre structure sits atop a pond in the middle of a housing estate, serving as kind of hybrid between building and public artwork. *Photo: James Hart*

Peterlee:

Flat rooves on homes was another common feature of 1950s and 1960s residential estates. Although cheaper to construct, especially on masse, than pitched roof housing, flat rooves had a tendency to amass rainwater, ultimately leading to growths of moss and grasses and problems with damp, rust and rot.

As such, many buildings in towns like Peterlee have had pitched rooves retrospectively added on, as clearly seen by the different coloured brickwork in this image (surrounding two-storey homes have been similarly treated).

Note also here the original low-pressure sodium street lighting which is still in situ in many northern towns. *Photo: Picnicin*.

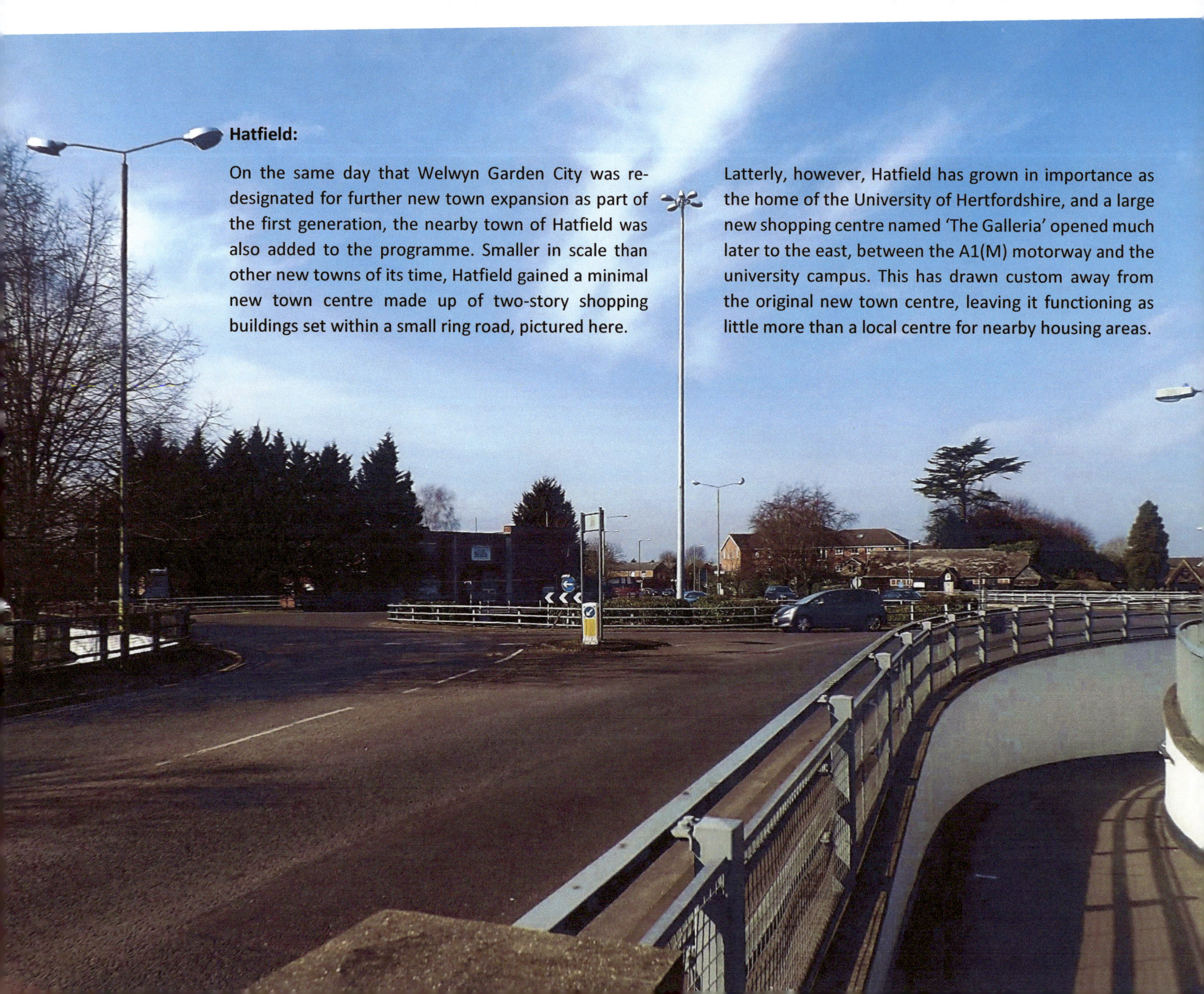

Hatfield:

On the same day that Welwyn Garden City was re-designated for further new town expansion as part of the first generation, the nearby town of Hatfield was also added to the programme. Smaller in scale than other new towns of its time, Hatfield gained a minimal new town centre made up of two-story shopping buildings set within a small ring road, pictured here.

Latterly, however, Hatfield has grown in importance as the home of the University of Hertfordshire, and a large new shopping centre named 'The Galleria' opened much later to the east, between the A1(M) motorway and the university campus. This has drawn custom away from the original new town centre, leaving it functioning as little more than a local centre for nearby housing areas.

Basildon:

Construction started on the second new town in Essex, Basildon, in 1951. Unlike most of the first generation, Basildon was not a significant centre prior to being designated as a new town. Instead the new town took its name from one of the small villages on the proposed site, something which would later be repeated by Milton Keynes.

Two pre-existing towns were incorporated in the new town area in the forms of Laindon and Pitsea. Both of these underwent considerable redevelopment in line with Basildon's principles, and little remains to identify them as distinct towns today.

The new town centre was placed roughly half way between the two existing centres. Built on a larger scale than those found in other first-generation towns, the centre features a number of high-rise buildings, a half-mile long central pedestrian street, two public gathering spaces and a sizeable indoor shopping complex, complemented by a large amount of smaller outdoor units.

A dual carriageway ring road completely encircles the town centre, with parking and bus facilities connected to this, allowing for a completely pedestrianised central area.

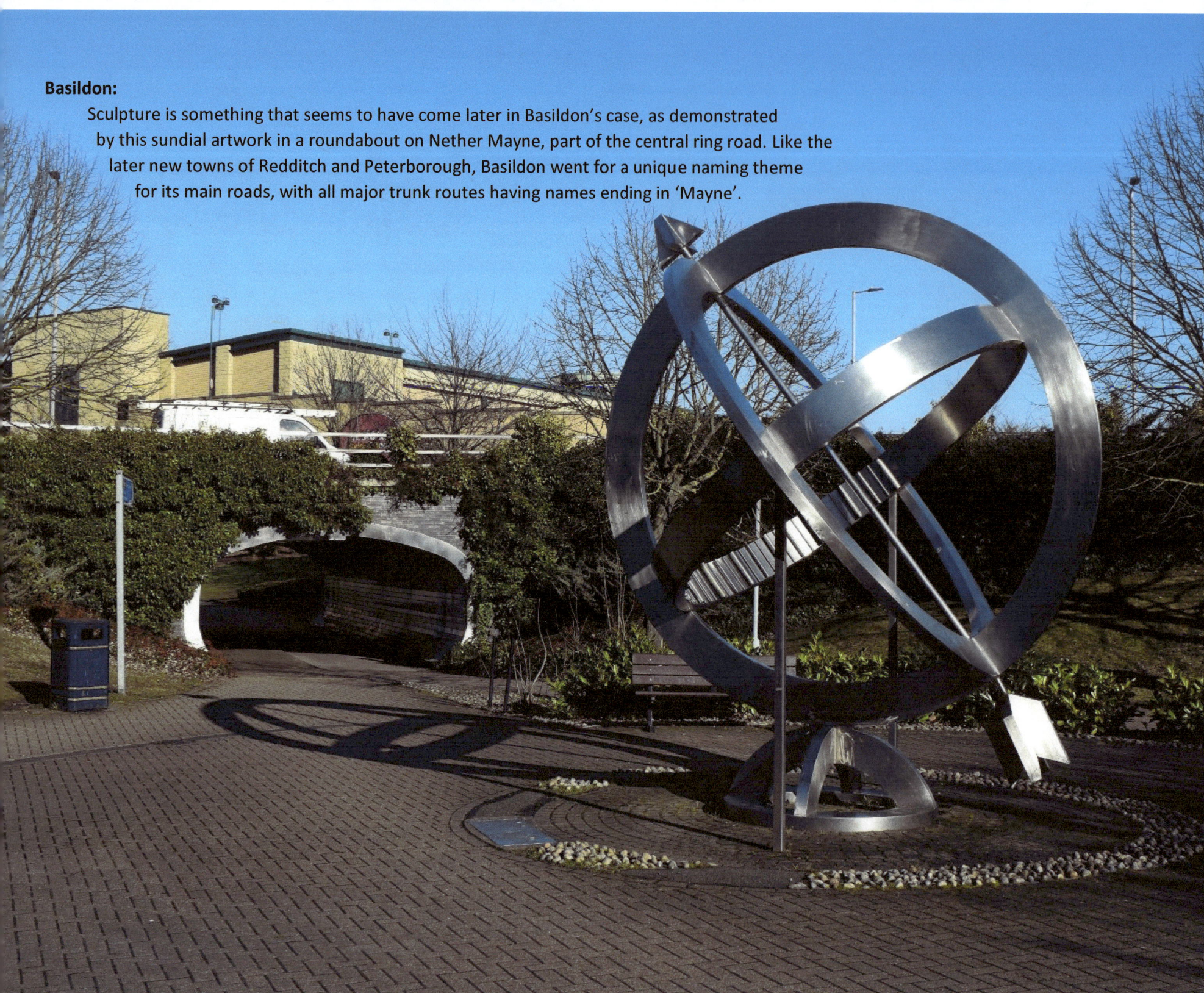

Basildon:

Sculpture is something that seems to have come later in Basildon's case, as demonstrated by this sundial artwork in a roundabout on Nether Mayne, part of the central ring road. Like the later new towns of Redditch and Peterborough, Basildon went for a unique naming theme for its main roads, with all major trunk routes having names ending in 'Mayne'.

Basildon:

Experimental architecture is also a theme in many new towns, but is especially prevalent in Basildon. Community centres were provided in many of the early housing developments, although usually combined into local centres unlike this free-standing one. Terraced housing like that seen in the background was employed extensively, with a wide variety of block layouts, building materials and densities being used.

Bracknell:

The 3M tower was the largest and most striking component of Bracknell's new town centre skyline. The now-demolished yellow block housed an indoor covered market, above which stood thirteen stories of offices. Also known as Winchester House, the building was already quite run down in this 2011 view and disappeared completely in 2015, in spite of a campaign by the amusingly named "Fellowship of Overbearing Large Structures" to retain it.

The market that formally sat under the building will move into a new market square in the 'Lexicon' development in the near future. This is another example of the current trend in early new towns towards more traditional urban form as modern-day planners, led on by the theories of new urbanism, attempt to retroactively convert these new towns back into something more conventional.

Bracknell:

The bi-level square shown on the previous page, taken in 2011, is now no more. "Life as it should be" exemplifies the direction taken in the redevelopment of so many of England's new towns: complete rebuilding without any regard for modern heritage.

Bracknell town centre has been the hardest hit of all by this policy. A masterplan was developed before the 2008 economic crisis, which is now slowly but finally being implemented, gradually removing what remains of the original plan.

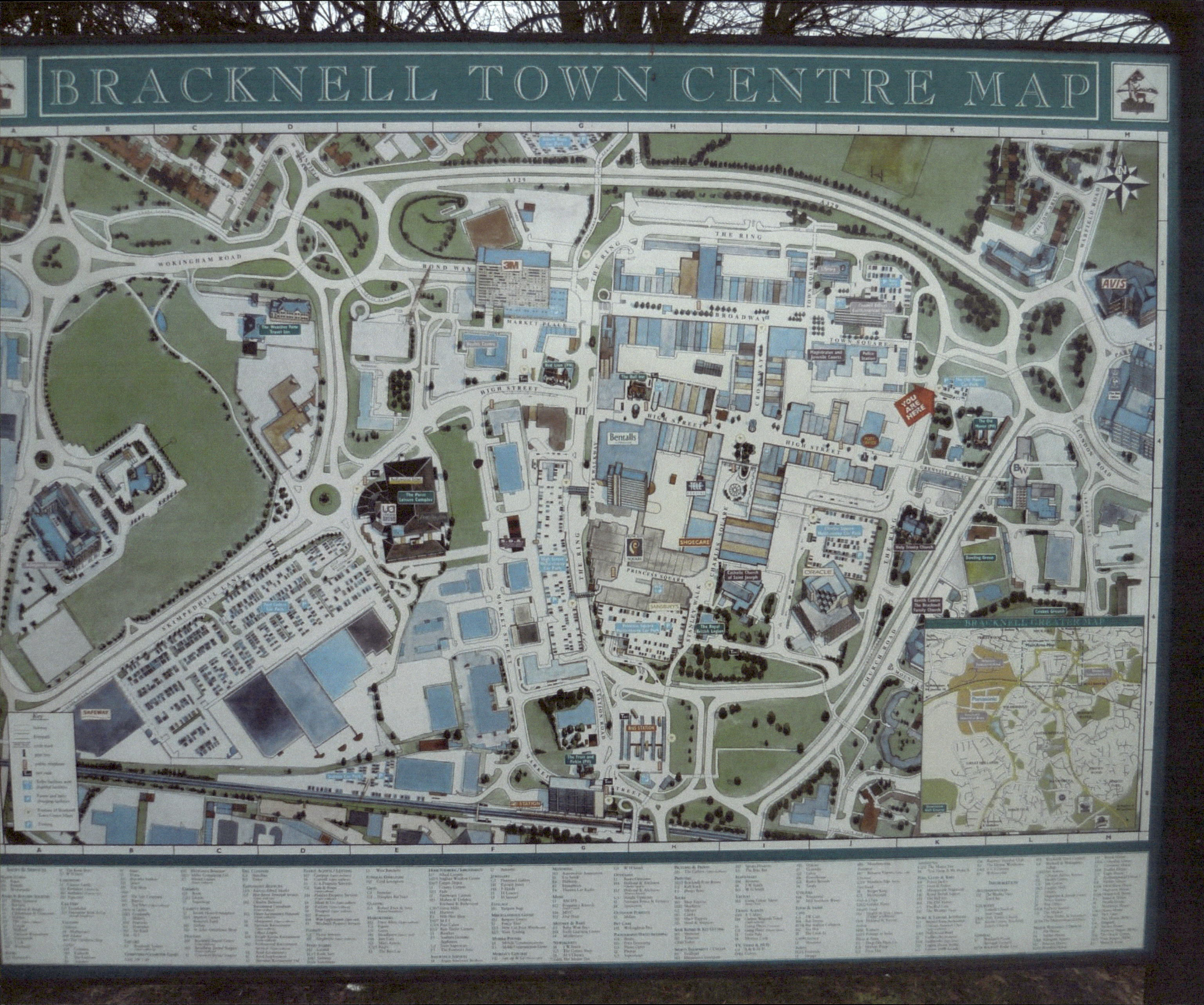
BRACKNELL TOWN CENTRE MAP
A329
THE RING
WOKINGHAM ROAD
BOND WAY
3M
MARKET PLACE
BROADWAY
TOWN SQUARE
HIGH STREET
Bentalls
SHOECARE
PRINCESS SQUARE
ORACLE
SKIMPEDHILL LANE
SAFEWAY
BUS STATION
CHURCH ROAD
LONDON ROAD
AVIS
YOU ARE HERE
BRACKNELL GREATER MAP

Corby:

Despite a stained reputation from the public health impact of a toxic waste spillage, Corby has gone on to enjoy something of a renaissance in recent years. What was once seen as an industrial town built around the steel industry is now marketed as a suburban commuter hub. It has even been somewhat laughably branded as 'North Londonshire' in recognition of its new intercity rail link to London, which reopened in 2009 after an abortive attempt at a passenger service to Kettering between 1987 and 1990.

The dramatic Corby Cube is the most striking example of the town's resurgence, featuring a theatre, library and council chambers. Alongside it are a new Olympic swimming pool and cinema, a far cry from the limited facilities of the original town centre. Much of that, including the old enclosed bus station, have disappeared under new shopping development.

Corby:

Underpasses are a very common and identifying feature of many new towns, and Corby is no exception. Something that particularly identifies earlier towns is the use of underpasses on relatively minor roads within housing developments. Small subways like this are common in Corby's older housing estates, whereas later towns used wider more bridge-like structures mainly for crossing major roads.

As can be seen, maintenance and upkeep has been poor in many of these areas, and some of Corby's original housing areas have been completely demolished and redeveloped with more modern higher density housing.

Corby:

Much of Corby's original housing stock demonstrates the mass-produced nature of social housing in the 1950s and 1960s. Footways and roads were segregated, with footpaths running around the housing blocks and under linkages between buildings, often creating circuitous routes for pedestrians. Desire lines would often form diagonally across green spaces or alongside arterial roads. A common criticism of new towns is that the segregation of walking routes away from roads makes them intimidating and unsafe for pedestrians, although the intention here was exactly the opposite. The thinking at the time was that running footpaths through housing rather than around it created more natural surveillance.

The Second Generation: 1961-1964

Although the first generation of new towns had done a lot to alleviate housing shortages around London and the south east of England, much of the poorer north of the country was still suffering from severe shortages and living in Victorian housing without modern facilities.

In response to this, a second wave of new towns was created between 1961 and 1964. These were clustered around the population centres of Birmingham, Liverpool and Newcastle.

There was little change in the urban and aesthetic design principles between the first and second generations. A little more ambition was applied in terms of scale and development of infrastructure, but by and large the same overall design ethic prevailed.

Unfortunately, as time has gone by some of these towns have struggled to succeed like their better-connected southern counterparts.

Skelmersdale:

The economic reality of a London-centric Britain has led to mixed fortunes for the new towns of Northern England, but nowhere quite embodies the struggles of northern new towns as well as Skelmersdale. The Lancashire town is essentially half-finished, with large amounts of the town still being undeveloped. Like elsewhere, a central covered shopping centre was created, surrounded by a ring road and connected by bridges and underpasses to some peripheral office development. To the west was an elevated bus station, linked in turn to a small pedestrian area, where facilities like a Library and civic buildings were provided.

Building work on "Skem" effectively stopped at the start of the 1980s. In a newly deregulated market the town struggled to attract interest from private developers, and to this day large parts of the town centre stand empty. Incomplete walkways end in muddy wasteland, while a large civic square is peppered with weeds and surrounded on all but one side by empty grassland and trees. Recent efforts have been made to 'regenerate', but attracting investment to this desolate part of western Lancashire still seems problematic.

Skelmersdale:

Perhaps the most distinctive feature of "Skem" is its gigantic roundabouts and half-finished road infrastructure. The town was clearly intended to be far larger than has actually been realised, and many of the roundabouts, such as 'Hope Island' featured here, include large reservations in the centre for unbuilt future flyovers. One of these is so huge it's earned the name 'Half Mile Island'. The town's northern areas are still incomplete, with roads and footpaths running into empty fields.

Skelmersdale:

Housing in Skelmersdale is very uniform, with developments throughout the town hung in small closes and courts on a framework of looping secondary roads that swing out from and re-join the main arteries. Like in earlier first-generation towns, footpaths run through and often beneath homes, usually away from roads and frequently switching to elaborate grade-separated crossings to get over both larger roads and smaller distributors. The housing here is somewhat more leafy than in earlier towns, with a system of suburban parks running between the housing estates, especially around the Birch Green district, linking into the Tawd Valley Park. Remarkably little later development has appeared, with the Ashurst estate to the north being the only sizeable district dating from the 1990s. This has left Skelmersdale as one of the best-preserved of all the original new towns, although with regeneration and a new rail link constantly in planning, that may not remain true for long.

Skelmersdale:

The designers of the new towns were seeking to create more than just population centres; a sense of 'place' was also at the forefront of the planners' minds. Generous amounts of public art were a notable feature in many instances, particularly in Skelmersdale, where artworks such as this are used to introduce personality and variation into what can otherwise be a very repetitive townscape.

Water features were also incorporated into the central shopping building, livening up the otherwise inactive frontages of the building around which service roads ran.

Redditch:

More attention seems to have been payed to the environment in the suburbs of Redditch than in those of other first and second generation new towns. Linear parks wind their way through the suburbs in a manner very similar to later third generation towns, and a lot of balancing lakes like this one are provided to protect against the risk of flooding. There are also several areas of woodland, lending the urban form a much more distributed and suburban feel than that in earlier towns.

Redditch:

A sign of changing times? A regeneration scheme has led to the bricking up of this underpass under Redditch's one-way inner ring road. Although these towns were designed with the long-term very much in mind, with futureproofing for envisaged population growth, times and trends change and the language of the original plan often comes into conflict with modern day planning needs and priorities. Like Skelmersdale, Redditch's road network is a lesson in futureproofing, featuring England's only American-style cloverleaf interchange (another exists in Livingstone near Edinburgh, another new town and subject of a possible future volume). Rail facilities in both Redditch and Skelmersdale are minimal, however.

Redditch:

For its suburban streets, Redditch adopted a similar style of street signage to that used in Crawley, but without the colour-coding for different estates. Under every street name, which is written in white against a blue background, the name of the estate is given in black on white.

Major through roads are given a more basic white-on-blue sign, seeing as they run between rather than through the estates. These roads are all named 'Highway', each being named after the destination the road runs towards.

Redditch is one of the few towns to use both a unique signage and road naming scheme. Similar signage systems exist in Crawley and Milton Keynes, while Basildon and Peterborough adopted similar naming systems.

Redditch:

Picking up on the public art theme, in many areas more recent public art has been used to brighten up areas perceived as unwelcoming or unattractive. This small underpass replaced a former road bridge over a railway line that originally ran south from the town towards Alcester and Evesham. These paintings have been applied to discourage graffiti tagging, a common problem on the large amounts of flat wall, concrete infrastructure and underpass structures found in most new towns. Interestingly, the underpass is built into a small section of the original railway bridge wall, just visible to the right. Rail transport was on the decline in the 1960s when new towns were being developed, and no thought was given to the possibility that these major new centres would need high quality rail links. As such, Redditch is stuck at the end of a single-track branch from Birmingham with no through links to the rest of the country.

Runcorn:

Like many earlier new towns, Runcorn created a new town centre separate to that of the original town. This was several miles away from the original riverside town centre, and as such was never able to truly replace it. Runcorn is still seen as retaining its original town centre today, and the new one has become known as 'Shopping City'. Shopping City also forms the heart of a unique bus-based mass transit system, the Runcorn Busway, which runs on segregated metro-like routes around all the new town development areas, switching to elevated lines through the centre. *Photo: Simon Smiler*

Runcorn:

Designed as an overspill town for an overcrowded and severely war-damaged Liverpool, Runcorn sat in the shadow of the original Runcorn Bridge, carrying both road and rail links across the Mersey. However in recent years this has become a bottleneck, resulting in a project to construct the Mersey Gateway Bridge. This new link, opened in 2017, ties directly into Runcorn's new town network of expressways, and actually refocuses the road network onto the 1960s town centre. Perhaps Shopping City will now finally start to be recognised as the centre of modern-day Runcorn.

The Third Generation: 1967-1970

The original New Towns Commission envisaged towns with populations of up to 60,000, but the last few entries into the original new towns programme were to be far, far larger, with populations envisaged of up to 300,000.

By the end of the 1960s both technology and society had moved on. The public was reacting against the brutalist movement and a more traditional approach to urban design was coming back into favour. The time was right for a return to the garden city concept.

The third-generation new towns fall into two broad categories. The first is comprised of the two completely new-build cities, Telford and Milton Keynes. The rest were expansions of existing significant urban centres, transforming market towns and small cities into huge urban centres. Although the names of some of these towns and cities have historical connotations, the urban centres we know today are a far cry from what existed prior to their designations.

Milton Keynes:

What really sets the third generation apart from what came before is the scale and vision that went into these towns. Nowhere is this more evident than in Milton Keynes, which made a conscious effort to get away from the repetitive style of earlier new towns and re-embrace Ebenezer Howard's Garden City principles, albeit on a far larger scale. Despite lacking the Royal Charter needed for city status, Milton Keynes is widely seen and referred to as a city to this day.

Milton Keynes:

Nothing says 'garden city' quite like a half mile-long expanse of open parkland. With hundreds of miles of new high-quality road infrastructure and housing being built, the construction of Milton Keynes created a vast amount of spoil. This was used to landscape an area to the east of the city centre into one of Britain's largest urban parks outside London. The park features a belvedere viewing point offering views across into Bedfordshire, ten miles to the east, as well as an assortment of lakes and ponds, areas of woodland and an 'events plateau' including an open-air amphitheatre. Development was envisaged to extend the city centre down both sides of the park, but these sites have remained vacant after plans to build them out in the 1990s fell through. However, in recent years work has finally begun on filling in these empty spaces to complete the original concept of a park within the city.

Milton Keynes:

At the new city's heart it was decided to build Europe's largest indoor shopping complex. Completed in 1979, the building was Grade II listed in 2012, with English Heritage drawing particular attention to the 'infinity views' along the building's half-mile long north and south facades.

Milton Keynes:

What's particularly singular about the largest of the new towns is the way that the self-proclaimed city's urban design has been recognised locally. Attempts to move to a more modern form of urbanism have been heavily resisted, resulting in brand new developments that still adhere to the MK Development Corporation's original design principles, like the Oakgrove development seen here, still under construction at the time of writing. The recent innovation of neighbourhood planning has led to even more protection for the city's heritage, along with the listing of several notable city centre buildings and the development of a local heritage register, protecting public spaces and assets as well as buildings.

Milton Keynes:

As well as returning to Ebenezer Howard's garden city principles, Milton Keynes also went right back to the origins of British new towns in one distinctive way: the grid layout. Roads are numbered V for 'Vertical' and H for 'Horizontal'.

Grids have a long history in city planning, with the 13th century Kent village of Winchelsea and the later planned centres of Edinburgh and Glasgow adopting grid layouts. However it was the influence of American cities like Los Angeles with their heavily engineered grid-based road systems that most influenced the Milton Keynes network. The last official extension to the system was in 2003, but this map adds more recent roads, notably the V12 "Fen Street", into the network.

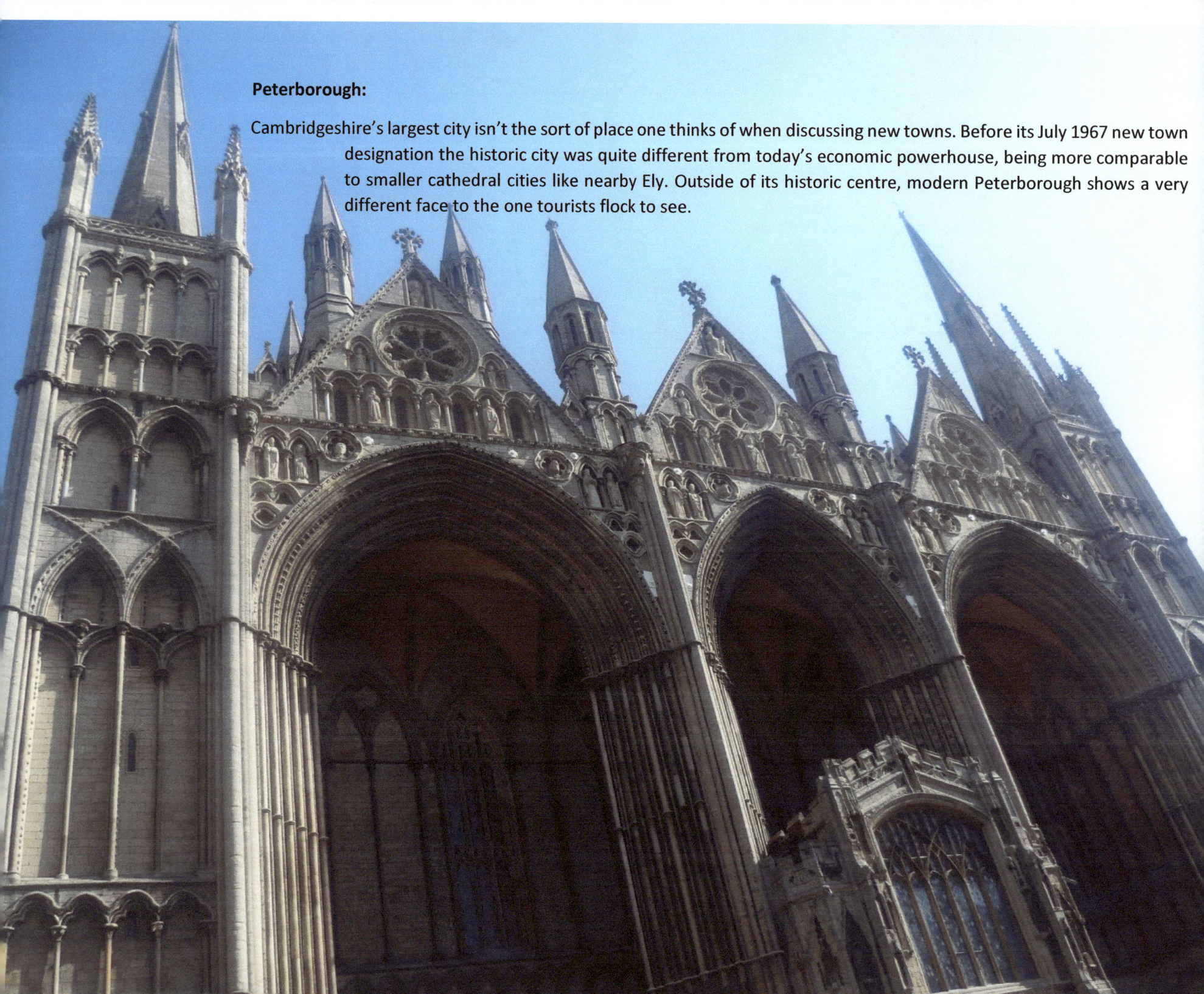

Peterborough:

Cambridgeshire's largest city isn't the sort of place one thinks of when discussing new towns. Before its July 1967 new town designation the historic city was quite different from today's economic powerhouse, being more comparable to smaller cathedral cities like nearby Ely. Outside of its historic centre, modern Peterborough shows a very different face to the one tourists flock to see.

Peterborough:

Like Milton Keynes, Peterborough also adopted a unique system for its intra-city road network. Here a network of 'Parkway' roads were constructed, named similarly to Redditch's 'Highways' after nearby towns and villages towards which they run. Peterborough's network was far more complete than that of many other new towns, with a system of fully grade-separated expressways serving the city.

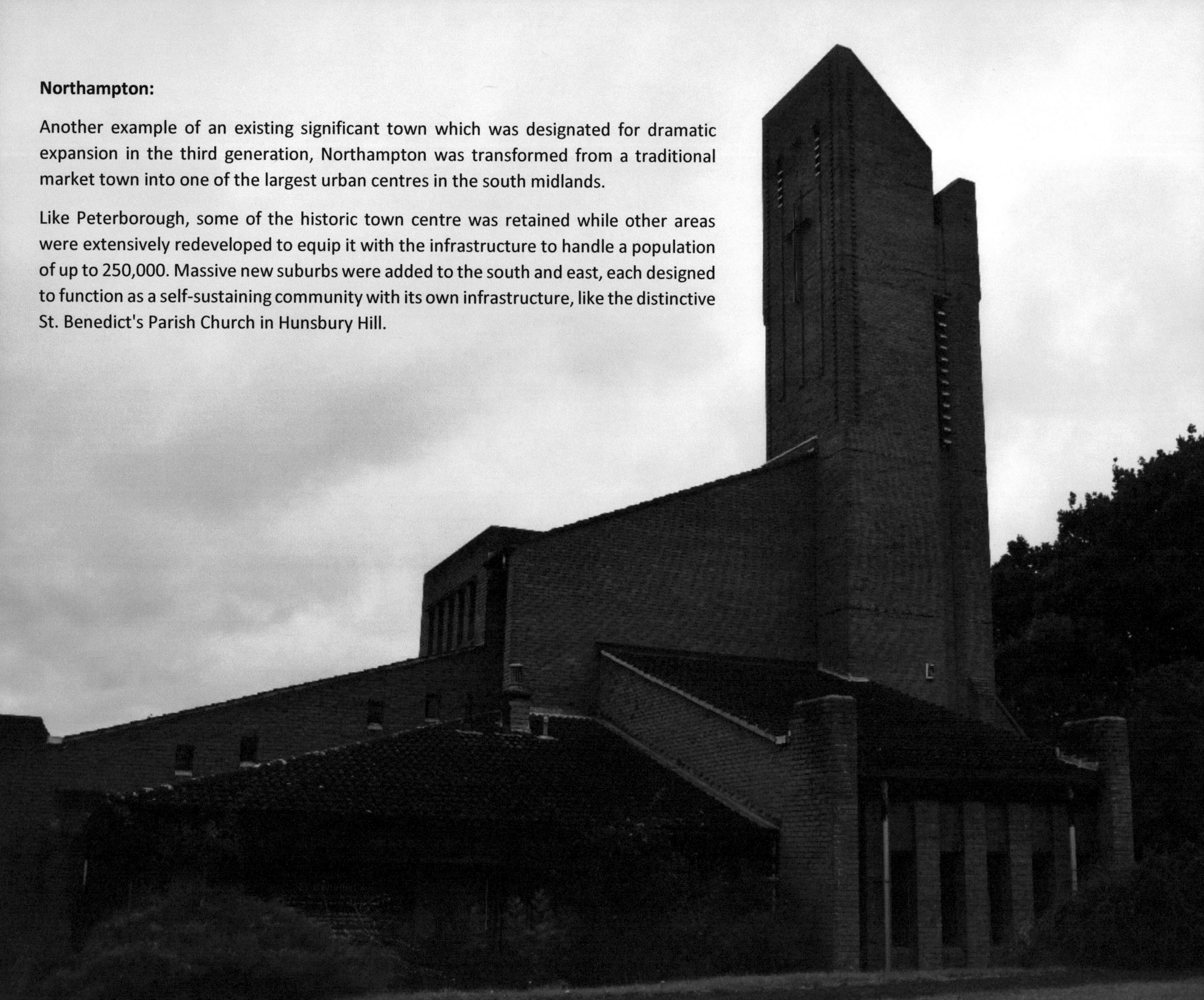

Northampton:

Another example of an existing significant town which was designated for dramatic expansion in the third generation, Northampton was transformed from a traditional market town into one of the largest urban centres in the south midlands.

Like Peterborough, some of the historic town centre was retained while other areas were extensively redeveloped to equip it with the infrastructure to handle a population of up to 250,000. Massive new suburbs were added to the south and east, each designed to function as a self-sustaining community with its own infrastructure, like the distinctive St. Benedict's Parish Church in Hunsbury Hill.

Northampton:

Perhaps the most distinctive landmark in Northamptonshire's county town is the Express Lift Tower. Built to the west of the town centre in the late 1970s, this concrete behemoth was used to test high-speed elevators for use in skyscrapers. Now a listed building, it finds itself today surrounded by more recent housing developments. Various proposals over the years to turn it into a viewing gallery or public attraction have yet to come to fruition.

The tower is known locally as the 'Northampton Lighthouse', referencing the fact that it can be seen from a considerable distance, especially to the west. This is particularly apparent to travellers passing on West Coast Main Line express trains, which bypass Northampton some five miles to the west thanks to resistance to the railway from local townspeople in the 19th century.

Like many things in Northampton, and arguably the town itself, the Express Lift Tower polarises opinion, with some considering it a defining landmark while others see it as an eyesore and a barrier to development.

Northampton:

The most striking contribution Northampton Development Corporation made to the town centre was the Greyfriars Bus Station. Set around a central island accessed from underground passageways, the station featured two roads down either side (the northern one is seen in this image). Buses could circulate around the station in this manner, allowing services to arrive and depart easily from any direction. The entire station was on a downhill slope from east to west, allowing the rolling wooden doors to self-close under gravity.

As is so often the case, the station was hated by many locals and acquired a reputation in later years for being damp, dirty, dark and unwelcoming. By 2014 a much smaller replacement bus station had been constructed with some controversy at North Gate. This has led to many services having to use the unprotected Drapery stops instead, whilst others have to go well out of their way to reach the poorly sited replacement station.

Despite attempts by local groups to get Greyfriars listed, the station was demolished completely later the same year. As of 2018 the site remains vacant and undeveloped.

Wellingborough:

Along with the designated new towns of Northampton and Corby, two other Northamptonshire towns were also expanded along similar principles: Daventry and Wellingborough. Both are smaller towns in the 20,000-30,000 population region, resulting in developments that seem quite over-engineered for towns of this size. Pictured below is the 1970s Nest Farm Estate in Wellingborough, which follows the same design principles as nearby Northampton's much larger "Eastern District".

Warrington:

A major centre of industrial development in the 19th century, Warrington was already a substantial town by the time it was designated as a new town in 1968. Its designation helped it stave off many of the effects of industrial decline that affected so many of England's northern cities, and today it has become a centre for technology and light industry. Many of the older industrial areas have been redeveloped as new town housing estates, but the new town design themes are really only found in the suburbs and there is little in the town centre to identify Warrington as anything other than a traditional northern industrial town.

Telford:

The only new town to come close to Milton Keynes in its ambition and scale is Telford. Actually designated under the second generation as Dawley New Town, inheriting its name from an existing local village, the town was re-designated under the third generation as Telford. Taking its new name from the famous local engineer Thomas Telford, the re-designated town encompassed a much larger area, incorporating the existing towns of Wellington and Oakengates and a number of smaller towns and villages. Despite its less advantageous location in rural Shropshire, Telford has gone on to overtake neighbouring Shrewsbury to become the largest urban centre in the county.

Telford:

Something that is often overlooked in the study of new town heritage is the unique designs of street lighting that were sometimes employed. While some earlier new towns created their own distinctive styles of signs to create distinctive character, some third-generation towns developed a complete language of street furniture.

Telford, along with Milton Keynes and parts of Skelmersdale, adopted the right-angled octagon-based style of lamppost shown here for their primary road networks. The deep-bowled low-pressure sodium lantern on the nearest column is typical of the lighting originally used, while the newer low-pressure lantern on the opposite side of the road and the high-pressure lanterns further in the distance on the left side are examples of later replacements. A recent drive towards greater energy efficiency has seen the implementation of LED lighting in many towns, replacing the deep orange glow of low-pressure sodium and the pinker hue of high-pressure sodium with a brighter white light.

Within housing areas, Telford used a smaller version of the octagonal steel column, either with a curved side arm or the lantern affixed directly to the top of the column, while Milton Keynes developed its own unique family of brown square-based columns with spherical lanterns. In both towns these have latterly been replaced with the standard wide-based circular columns found elsewhere.

Telford:

As well as street lighting, Telford had its own family of signage for roads and footways. The metallic signage reflected the history of the area, with Thomas Telford's famous iron bridge being to the south of the new town. These signs were finished off with a circular totem on the top, but as is so often the case, some have started to disappear and be replaced by more off-the-shelf products. Maintaining these unique features often presents a headache for today's local authorities.

A number of new towns used signs like this to add character to their settlements, including the blue and white fingerposts of the Milton Keynes 'redway' network and the colour-coded estates of Crawley. In Telford, however, there was a subtle attempt to acknowledge heritage which was absent in many other towns, and the design of the central shopping building also pays homage to the iron bridge and Telford's other works in its design motifs.

Telford:

The facilities provided in Telford's new town centre were a little basic in nature, especially given the size of the town. The bulk of the town's civic heart is contained within a single shopping building encircled by a one-way ring road. On the edges are a few small appending buildings such as this library and the very memorably named 'Meeting Place House'. Much of the development around the centre is isolated office buildings, with a large town park to the south and a lot of still undeveloped land immediately to the west. Adding variety and scale to the town centre has been a challenge as Telford has grown into Shropshire's largest urban area, and the new Southwater development has introduced an outdoor shopping street and a range of new leisure and cultural facilities.

Central Lancashire:

Preston's historic high street may seem like a strange place for the story of the New Towns Programme to end, but the fact is that Britain's last true new town was something of an abortive project. The unimaginatively named "Central Lancashire New Town" was grand in scale at the outset. A new agglomeration of Preston, Chorley and Leyland housing 300,000 people was envisaged, filling in the space between the existing centres in a similar manner to how Milton Keynes filled in the space between Bletchley, Newport Pagnell and Wolverton. What was ultimately delivered, however, was a series of urban extensions of the existing towns with no real linkages between them. The Central Lancashire Development Corporation was wound up in 1986, bringing an unceremonious end to a broadly unsuccessful project. Little exists to identify Central Lancashire as a new town beyond some areas on the west side of Chorley, particularly the Chancery Road estate, which betray their true heritage.

Outside the Programme

The first two generations of the new towns programme took a very geographic approach, locating the new settlements close to major existing centres (London and Newcastle for the first generation, Liverpool and Manchester for the second). However, some local authorities outside these areas also decided to embark on major expansions of towns in their areas along the same development principles.

Some of these towns, especially Basingstoke, are often mistaken for new towns in their own right. Many experienced comprehensive redevelopment of their town centres to cater for an enlarged population, while suburban areas adopted a similar car-dominant layout and bulk-built social housing structure as the first two generations of the New Towns Programme.

There are many examples of this kind of development in older towns, but the examples shown here represent the most significant application of new town principles to towns outside the program.

Basingstoke:

A recurring theme in England's new towns, especially those inspired by the garden cities movement, was the use of low densities and low building cities to create 'cities in the forest', blending the urban and natural worlds with 'no building taller than the tallest tree'. However other towns designated for large scale expansion at the same time did not have development corporations and as such were less constrained by these principles.

The aversion to tall buildings was entirely absent in Hampshire's Basingstoke. In the 1960s the town embarked on a dramatic expansion plan as part of the London Overspill project, which included adding an expanded town centre to the north of the existing high street.

As the town trebled its population some of the employment need was met through an area of very large-scale office development in the town centre and eastwards alongside the railway. Numerous buildings of between 10 and 20 stories were constructed along Basing View, some of which have since been demolished. Many remain, including this distinctive Barclays headquarters which overlooks the large Eastrop Roundabout.

Basingstoke:

Many of the principles of the new towns programme can be found in overspill towns like Basingstoke, including a large amount of open space. Eastrop Park, seen here, is one of several small areas of parkland that pepper the estates around the town. However there is no interlinked consistent parks system like those found in most new towns, and the built form is mostly unbroken from one side of the town to the other.

For its new road network Basingstoke constructed a single ring of dual carriageway named 'Ringway', connected to the M3 Motorway in the southeast corner. Junctions were provided with scope for future grade-separation, but in practise many have remained as oversized roundabouts with space for future flyovers. An additional section of dual carriageway bisects the centre of the ring through the new part of the town centre.

Andover:

A historic market town dating back to before the Doomsday Book, Andover started taking large amounts of London Overspill development in the 1950s. Today the classic town centre is surrounded by newer development and a network of fast main roads and large roundabouts rivalling that of any new town.

Droitwich Spa:

A minor Worcestershire town until the 1960s home to only a few thousand people, Droitwich was, along with nearby Bromsgrove, earmarked for large amounts of Birmingham overspill development. A large area to the west of the town was developed with social and later private housing, very much along new town design lines, divided from the old town by a new bypass on the A38. Landscape parkland along the canal and river routes and two industrial areas were also built. The town, now transformed almost beyond recognition, continues to grow to this day, with new development continuing to the south.

Swindon:

The historical home of the Great Western Railway doesn't seem like a likely subject for inclusion in this book, but it has a lot in common with some of the third generation new towns. Following rail nationalisation, its importance as an industrial centre went into decline, while its resident population went the other way.

As a result, a growth programme began in the 1950s which included comprehensive redevelopment of the town centre and massive expansion to the north, west and southeast. Today's glass, concrete and steel town centre is easily mistaken for those of Basildon or Crawley, while the suburbs lack the landscaping of many new towns but clearly share their approach to movement and design.

Tamworth:

Perhaps the town most often mistaken for a member of the new towns programme, Tamworth had a completely new boundary established in the 1960s to cater for Birmingham overspill development. Social housing estates like Belgrave, pictured here, were developed for the new population with the same segregated layout as used in first and second generation towns like Corby and Skelmersdale.

Tamworth:

A massive road building programme accompanied the expansion, with a new 'through-pass' expressway section of the A5 built around Wilnecote (very similar to the A5 through Milton Keynes) and several dual and single carriageway main roads, segregated from pedestrian routes, linking this to the town centre and new housing areas. The town centre was augmented with new shopping areas, but otherwise the local heritage was respected, with the castle and historic town centre churches and shopping streets left largely unchanged. This is in contrast with some new towns like Redditch, where wholesale demolition of streets and buildings caused severe local controversy.

The Next Generation

The designation of the Central Lancashire new town in 1970 brought an end to the creation of new settlements under the new towns programme. In recent decades, however, the concept of new settlements to tackle a growing population has begun to re-emerge, albeit with very different planning and design principles to those of the classic new towns.

In the 1990s and 2000s 'sustainable urban extensions' became a popular concept. These self-sufficient mini-towns like Fairford Leys on the edge of Aylesbury or Poundbury on the edge of Dorchester mirrored the design ethic of traditional market towns, forgoing a focus on movement and replacing it with one on the pedestrian experience.

Smaller new towns have been a popular proposal recently, with a series of 'eco-towns' on similar lines to Cambourne in Cambridgeshire proposed before the 2008 financial crisis. These latter-day 'new towns' really bare no relation to the older subjects of this volume, but I include some examples by way of contrast to illustrate just how much planning ethics have changed in the modern era.

Fairford Leys:

The concept of expanding existing towns fell out of favour towards the end of the 1990s, with planners moving towards creating independent new settlements loosely associated with the larger towns they adjoin. Fairford Leys and Poundbury were early examples of these 'urban extensions', built along traditional principles as standalone towns with their own clearly defined centres.

Fairford Leys:

These 'towns' essentially tested the water for what would become the next generation of real new towns. With an emphasis on sustainability, these established a very different rulebook from that of the original new towns programme. The car is at the bottom of the hierarchy now, with the focus placed squarely on creating comfortable, intimate environments for residents and pedestrians. Buses and cycles are given favour over cars. Despite its attempt at traditional design, Fairford Leys has gained an unfavourable reputation in adjoining Aylesbury for being impossible to navigate and lacking character. It would seem that neither the open rebellion of the original new towns against traditional design, nor this attempt to emulate it, have succeeded in achieving that indefinable quality of being characterful.

Cambourne:

Construction started on Britain's first true new town since 1970 in 1998 on open countryside midway between Cambridge and St. Neots. Rather than one integral town, Cambourne is built as three closely connected 'villages', named Upper, Lower and Great Cambourne. These are clustered around a central high street, shown here, with a very modest set of facilities including a pub, a small public square and a supermarket. A separate employment area is also provided between the three villages and the A428 expressway.

Cambourne:

The only real link between Cambourne and the original new towns is the use of the 'redway' combined foot/cycle path concept, developed for Milton Keynes and later introduced in other towns around the country. Twenty years after work started, the final of the three villages is now nearing completion, and plans are afoot to add a fourth, larger element to the town. This is despite the fact that Cambourne, by design, lacks infrastructure to handle a larger population and the traffic and service demand that will bring. This approach nearly continued with the abortive "eco towns" programme of the late 2000s. Let's hope any further new towns are built with the infrastructure to support their growth.

Index of Towns and Cities

Andover	-65.
Aylesbury	-70-71.
Basildon	-23-25.
Basingstoke	-63-64.
Bracknell	-26-29.
Cambourne	-73-74.
Central Lancashire	-61.
Chorley	-61.
Corby	-30-32.
Crawley	-13-14.
Dawley	-57-60.
Droitwich Spa	-66.
Fairford Leys	-70-71.
Harlow	-18-19.
Hemel Hempstead	-15-17.
Hertford	-22.
Letchworth Gdn City	-5-7.
Milton Keynes	-45-49.
Northampton	-52-54.
Peterborough	-50-51.
Peterlee	-20-21.
Preston	-61.
Redditch	-38-41.
Runcorn	-42-43.
Skelmersdale	-34-37.
Stevenage	-11-12.
Swindon	-67.
Tamworth	-68-69.
Telford	-57-60.
Warrington	-56.
Wellingborough	-55.
Welwyn Garden City	-5, 8-9.

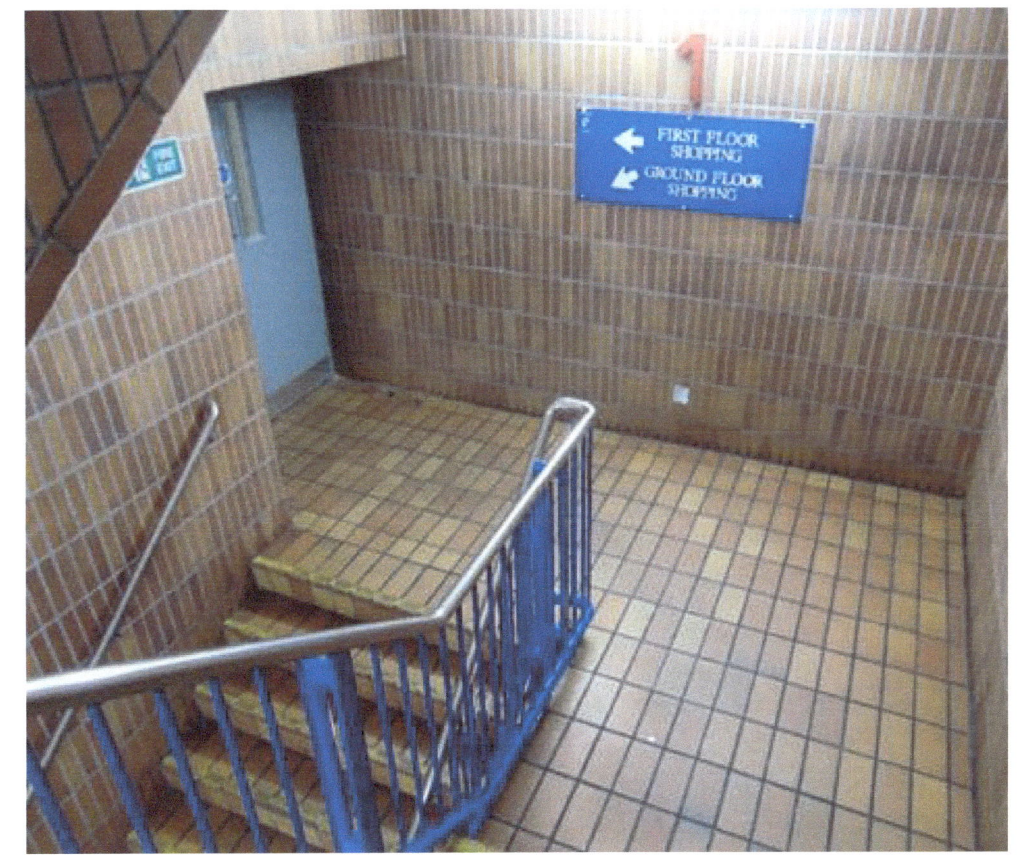

www.ingramcontent.com/pod-product-compliance
Lightning Source LLC
Chambersburg PA
CBHW041818080526

44587CB00004B/137